Where's Doopey?

Where's Doopey?

George L. Bushong

VANTAGE PRESS
New York

Illustrated by Kate Gartner

FIRST EDITION

Published by Vantage Press, Inc.
516 West 34th Street, New York, New York 10001

Manufactured in the United States of America
ISBN: 0-533-09435-6

Library of Congress Catalog Card No.: 90-90387

0 9 8 7 6 5 4 3 2 1

To my daughter, Bonnie Jeanne

Contents

Preface

The story I am about to tell you took place several years ago, and was told to me at the end of each day as it happened. I will try to recall all of the events as they occurred, although occasionally there may be omissions because of the lapse of time, but these should not directly affect the story. At the time I remember it became increasingly difficult to wait until the close of day when I knew that I would hear another chapter in the lives of the quaint friends that the little girl had become so attached to.

Also, with each succeeding day, the doubts I had concerning these quaint people began to diminish until finally I realized that no five-year-old girl could possibly have the imagination to create them and their predicaments. In fact, I often found myself wandering around the neighborhood, sometimes to the vacant lot; and even on two occasions, part-way into the dense woods in hope that maybe I could find the missing Doopey or perhaps come upon one of his friends. I never had that good fortune. However, had I been back in my childhood, my quest might not have been in vain.

I would also like to add that at that time, the little girl made me promise that I would never tell a "human bean" any of the story you are about to read. Recently, on reaching the mature age of twelve, she recalled those exciting days and decided it would be unfair not to share her experiences with other girls and boys.

Where's Doopey?

Introduction

"Let the meeting come to order."

The speaker was Indian Gook, sergeant-at-arms, of the Jolly Club. Indian Gook was very tall and very wide. He was indeed quite huge. His hands and feet were immense and seemed even larger in proportion to his giant frame. He was very clumsy-looking, and his actions did not belie his looks. Indian Gook never spoke, he always boomed.

"Let the meeting come to order," boomed Indian Gook.

There was a shrill scream from the other side of the club room. The scream came from Mary Jane, the club president.

"Just a minute," screamed Mary Jane. "I am president and I will call the meeting to order."

"We will now call the roll," boomed Indian Gook.

"Yes, we certainly will," screamed Mary Jane and she proceeded to call the roll.

"Upsty?"

"Here."

"Doopey?"

No answer.

"Doopey?" again but much louder.

Again no answer.

"Glass?"

"Here," answered Glass.

"Toasty?"

"Here."

"Indian Gook?"

"Here," boomed the Gook.

"Mary Jane?"

No answer and she repeated it much louder.

"Mary Jane?"

Suddenly realizing it was herself she was calling, she meekly whispered, "Here."

Mary Jane believed that the meetings should be conducted in a businesslike manner, and now she was quite annoyed as she noticed that Toasty and Upsty were paying little attention to what was going on at the meeting. Toasty was either laughing or giggling, and Upsty was smiling sagely. Mary Jane noticed all of this and wondered what was going on.

"Pray tell," said Mary Jane, "just what is going on?"

Toasty paid no attention to the president but turned to the others. "I just have to tell you what happened today," he said. He didn't wait for coaxing from his friends but continued right along. "You know," he said, "there's a special secret path that runs between the high road and the low road on the other side of Miller's Farm right on the edge of the woods. Today I'm coming along there and I can't wait to get to the peach tree that is partly

inside the farm and partly outside. Naturally when I get there and climb the tree, I climb the part of the tree that is outside of the farm. Well, I'm halfway up looking for a nice red ripe peach, and I see a couple of real ripe ones away up—but wait, what's this—am I seeing things, for right above the peaches is a branch—loaded with purple fruit."

Toasty paused to catch his breath and to see what effect this startling statement had on his listeners. Then he continued. "Yes, I said purple and this was a peach tree and without the impression of a doubt, I see what they are. They're plums."

There were gasps of astonishment now from the members of the club.

The first one to speak was Indian Gook. "You expect us to believe that?" he boomed.

"Unregardless of whether you believe it or not, it's for true," said Toasty.

"There was a whole branch full and when I finally got up enough nerve to taste one and was enjoying it, I heard someone coming down the path singing 'Can She Bake a Cherry Pie?' I knew it was Upsty and said to myself, 'Here's where I have some fun.' I picked another plum and slid down the tree just as Upsty was about to pass. 'What have you got there?' is his greeting. 'A plum,' says I, taking a small bite. 'And where in the world did you get a plum?' asks Upsty. 'Right up there,' says I, and all you could see from the ground were peaches. Upsty's mouth fell open and he whispered,

'Toasty, come with me, this is most amazing.' I was so surprised by Upsty's actions that I meekly followed him down the path that winds around Miller's orchard. I'm puffing along, for Upsty is walking very fast and when he had gone about a hundred yards, suddenly he stops and looks up into a big apple tree that I had often climbed before. 'Look up there,' he says to me and I look up and what do you think I see?"

"More plums, I guess," snorted the Gook.

"More plums is for true," replied Toasty. "I am sure this is a dream when Upsty pulls me aside. 'We had better not tell anyone about this,' he cautions. 'But, Upsty,' I stammer, 'we could make a fortune.' 'How?' asks Upsty, 'these are not our trees.' 'But regardless,' I come back, 'we could buy the Miller farm.' 'With what?' asks Upsty, and then he started to laugh so hard and so long that I thought these strange happenings had affected his brain. Then suddenly I knew what had happened. Upsty had taken the trouble to wire plum branches onto the peach and apple tree."

Toasty stopped talking now. He had finished his story, and all of his friends agreed that Upsty had indeed played a wonderful practical joke. They all laughed heartily, and Upsty and Toasty joined them.

"What did you do with all the plums?" asked Glass after the laughter had subsided. Glass was never at a loss for words where food was concerned.

“Left them right there for Mr. Miller to discover,” said Upsty, and there was more laughter.

Now all of the time that Toasty was relating his experience, Mary Jane was fidgeting around waiting for the story to be finished. Mary Jane did not have a sense of humor. She laughed politely with the others, but she really did not see anything so funny. They were here for a meeting, and it was her duty as president to see that the business part of the meeting came first.

Mary Jane rose from her chair.

“Now that Toasty has told his funny story,” she said, “let us proceed with the meeting. We had just completed calling the roll, and all were present and accounted for.”

“Yes,” parroted Indian Gook, “all present. Let’s proceed with the meeting.”

“Just a moment. Haven’t you forgot something? Or rather someone?”

All the members turned and stared at Upsty who had just spoken.

“I don’t think,” Upsty said, “that our good friend Doopey answered the roll call.”

Immediately it was apparent that Upsty was right.

“He didn’t, that’s for sure,” said Toasty, his voice a little shaky.

Upsty noticed that his friends were quite concerned about Doopey’s absence.

“Come, let’s be calm,” he said. “After all, Doopey might just be late.”

Glass said, "Doopey is never late."

Mary Jane echoed this statement, adding, "Especially for a meeting."

Toasty added, "Especially for a meeting to plan the Happy Day party."

Now all of the members began talking at once. What should be done in this emergency? And the babbling became louder and louder and how thunderous it might have become will never be known, for suddenly there was a loud banging against the clubhouse door. Immediately the hubbub inside shut off like a spigot and absolute quiet took its place.

Finally it was Indian Gook who broke the silence.

"What was that?" his brilliant question was put in a quavering boom.

"Open the door and see," said Upsty.

"No, no," cried Mary Jane. "It might be poor Doopey's body."

"Nonsense," said Upsty. "Toasty, you open the door."

Toasty pushed his chair toward the back of the room, hollering, "Glass, you're closer, you open it."

Just then a faint crying sound was heard outside of the door and Upsty, who could stand no more suspense, hurried over to open the door.

"Be sure to get the password," boomed Indian Gook.

Upsty was already unlatching the door and paid no attention to this warning.

When the door was opened, a cry went up from the members, for there at the bottom of the slight grade that led up to the clubhouse was a little girl. It was apparent at first look that she was pretty with blond curly hair and big blue eyes and on this occasion fresh scratches on the side of her face.

"Oh!" cried Mary Jane. "It's a little girl, and she's hurt. Bring her in, Upsty."

And Upsty brought the little girl in.

Now Mary Jane got some warm water and gently daubed the scratches on the little girl's face. The little girl cried some while this was being done, but soon she was all right and smiling at the strange-looking people around her.

Now Indian Gook decided to be the host.

"What's your name, little girl?" he boomed.

"Bonnie," came the answer. She spoke a little shakily. She was awed by the size of her questioner.

"Bonnie, huh?" the booming continued. "Is that all, just Bonnie?"

"No, no, it's Bonnie Jeanne," she said falteringly and looking around the room. She felt somewhat better as she saw the friendly looks on the faces of the other members.

"That's a funny name," thundered Indian Gook. "I never heard of Jeanne for a last name."

"Jeanne is not my last name," cried the little girl. "Jeanne is the last name of my first name. Brown is my very last name."

"Very confusing, very confusing indeed," boomed the Gook. "Where do you live?"

"In the white house 'cross the street," she whispered.

"You mean the brown house?"

"No, no, the white house," she cried.

"Now let's get this straight," boomed Indian Gook. "Your name is Brown, so it's the brown house or is it possible that your name is really White? That's it, you're probably a spy and your real name is White."

"My name is Brown," cried the little girl. "I'll tell my mommie, I will, I will," and now the tears were coming fast.

This was too much for Upsty. He had remained silent long enough. And when Upsty became excited, he often talked in rhymes and now he did. "Gook," he said, "if you go on to tease her, I will bop you on the beezer, that is if you'd get much smaller, and the Lord would make me taller."

So saying, Upsty now turned his attention to the newcomer. "What a pretty little girl," he said kindly, "and what pretty blue eyes. How old are you, Bonnie?"

"Just five," said the little girl.

"And do you go to school?"

Before she could answer, Glass, who could see that the little girl was about to be another one of Upsty's small admirers, went over and took her by the hand. "Come with me," said Glass, "I want to show you Upsty's poemtree." Glass led the little girl over to a corner of the room. There she saw an enormous tree, so big that it touched the ceiling

and so big that the little girl wondered why she hadn't noticed it before.

"It's lovely," she said, "but what are all of those pieces of paper hanging all over it?"

"They are Upsty's poems," said Glass. "Pick one off and read it."

The little girl reached up and picked a small piece of paper from the tree, but then she confessed she couldn't read. Upsty had followed them over to the poemtree and said that he could read the poem.

Then he started to laugh. "My gracious," Upsty said, "you would pick that one." Upsty laughed some more and then he read this poem:

> It's easy enough to be pleasant
> With nothing but dough in your purse
> But the man worth while
> Is the man who can smile
> As he takes that last ride in a hearse.

The little girl was not overly impressed with this work of art and hoped that there were better ones on the poemtree. Glass assured her that there were, and then Toasty came up with a brilliant idea.

"I have a brilliant idea," Toasty said. "The little girl is just like a fairy princess. Let's call her the Princess."

"Princess, Princess," cried Mary Jane. "That's what we'll call her," and all of the members started dancing around singing "Princess, Princess," and

Bonnie Jeanne was smiling and seemed real happy with her new friends.

Now it was Mary Jane's turn to have an idea, and she proposed that they make the princess a member of the club. "We'll make it real formal like and even initiate her."

"I don't want to be 'nitiated," cried the princess as she headed apprehensively toward the clubhouse door.

"Now, now," soothed Upsty, "there won't be any initiation." He turned to Mary Jane. "As president of the club, you should know that the princess is too young to be a member. However, there is nothing in the by-laws that says we can't start a junior membership."

Mary Jane thought that was a great idea, but Indian Gook, who had been silent for quite a while, boomed out "I still think she's a spy."

"Nonsense," cried Toasty, "she's no spy. She's one of those taxsquirts."

"Taxsquirts!" exclaimed Upsty. "What in the name of St. Pete is a taxsquirt?"

"Well, it's like this," Toasty was ready to expound. "There are those little shavers that roam the streets by the millions while Mom works to make up for the tax that is taken from pop's pay. The princess is definitely a taxsquirt."

This statement brought forth another outburst from the princess. "I am not no such thing," she cried. "I'm a 'Merican and I'll tell my mommie, that's what I'll do."

This was getting to be quite a meeting in the clubhouse. Like a day in April, showers, then clear skies, and now another storm brewing. Upsty had had enough of this inclemency and decided to act before the rains came again.

"Fellow members and you, dear princess, I have a suggestion to make. Suppose we," but that was as far as Upsty got. No one ever found out what the suggestion was going to be, for a loud ringing sound startled the occupants of the clubhouse.

"What's that, what's that?" screamed Indian Gook.

The ringing sound came again, and now bedlam really took over.

"What is it?"

"It's in here."

"It's out there."

"It's a bomb."

"It's the end of the world."

Suddenly Upsty remembered that a telephone had been installed earlier that morning, and much to the amazement of his friends, he calmly walked across the room and answered it.

"Hello," he said, "this is Upsty."

The voice he heard was deep and sounded ominous.

"You will never see your friend Doopey alive again." That was all. There was a click at the other end of the wire, and Upsty looked at his friends. His face was white.

"The news I heard now brings much sorrow. Let's adjourn now 'till the morrow." So saying, Upsty started for the door, but, of course, his friends wouldn't let him go until he told them of the strange and eerie phone call. Then, after much exclaiming, they dispersed, making arrangements to meet the next day, feeling terrible about Doopey, and how they had forgotten him with the excitement over the princess.

Play Ball

Let us imagine this beautiful summer day. It's quite early in the morning. You are standing in a field, or rather a lot, big enough for young boys to play baseball, and they do every chance they get. On the farther end of the lot, you see a group of tall trees that shade a small brook and neighboring parents often gather their children and picnic there on hot summer days. If you went not too far beyond these trees, you would enter a dense woods and, it is said, that you could walk for miles and miles through these woods, up and down hills and over many streams. It is also said that some peculiar gnomelike creatures once lived in these woods.

If you turned around and faced the other way, and threw a baseball maybe a little too hard, it would probably bounce over the street you see in the near distance and up onto the lawn of one of the row houses. These houses are pretty much alike except that one of them has recently been finished in a sparkling coat of white paint.

Halfway between you and the street, you see a sorry-looking shack that must be an eyesore to the people living in the row houses. Evidently some workmen, probably those who built the houses years ago, had put it together, chiefly with

Coca-Cola signs here and there, as though not to show discrimination, a few Pepsi-Cola signs. There it stood or leaned for years. The workmen had gone away, and nobody had ever bothered to tear it down.

Now if you were a little girl of five, you might see a short, sandy-haired character trudging toward the old shack. He had come from the direction of the woods. Then if you were a little girl of five, you would see the little fellow rub his palm on the weather-beaten door and, like sesame, it opens.

The little girl who lives in the newly painted house across the street from the sorry-looking shack was up quite early on this particular morning. She was on the front porch, playing with her favorite dolls, and happened to look over toward the old shack and saw Upsty. She was sure it was Upsty, going through the weather-beaten door.

The little girl crossed the street and went to the door of the old shack, which she was surprised to see was slightly ajar, so she tiptoed in. Inside she could find no one and was about to leave when she decided to go over and look at the poemtree. Then she saw Upsty. He was curled up in a giant chair behind the tree and was sound asleep and snoring away. But then the little girl saw something very startling. While there was no doubt that Upsty was sound asleep, oddly his right hand was wide awake, because it kept writing on a pad on Upsty's lap. The little girl watched intrigued, and there was no doubt that Upsty was writing away while deep in slumberland.

Finally Upsty sat up and slowly searched the room with misty eyes. When he saw the little girl, he became very excited and cried out, "Princess, Princess." Then Upsty told the little girl he had been dreaming about her, and usually the dream meant another poem for his poemtree. "Let's see what happened this time," he said to the princess and looked at the paper on his lap. "Oh! This is about you, Princess, and we will hang it on the poemtree. But first let me read it to you." And Upsty read the following:

> Where did you come from little girl?
> Did you parachute down on a golden curl?
> Did skates of silver speed your way?
> Did you glide in on the break of day?
> Don't answer me if you don't want to,
> But where did you get those eyes of blue?
> Did you come at dawn? Did you come at night?
> Did you come at noon when the sky was bright?
> Did you come in the showers on an April day?
> Did you come with the flowers in the month of May?
> Don't answer me if you don't want to,
> But where did you get those eyes of blue?
> Did you come from the home of the Eskimo
> Or the place where lotus blossoms grow?
> Or the land of the sphinx and the pyramid?
> Did you come alone? Of course you did.
> There couldn't be another just like you.
> Say where did you get those eyes of blue?

First Quarter

Now, all of the members were trooping into the clubhouse, and Mary Jane was reminding them that the meeting was of utmost importance. They had to do everything possible to find the missing Doopey. Upsty went over to the poemtree and hung up his latest creation, inspired by the little girl, and Indian Gook noticing this saw that the little girl was still in the clubhouse and tagging after Upsty every step he took. Indian Gook boomed out that he thought the stranger should leave while they were having their serious discussions. But Upsty and Toasty thought there was no harm in allowing her to stay and the others agreed.

Now Mary Jane called the meeting to order and after all of the formalities that are necessary on these occasions, she asked if anyone had any ideas that they could use to try and solve their problem. The problem being, of course, to find the missing Doopey.

There was an abundance of silence, and the members looked at each other as if each member was a prime suspect in the mysterious disappearance.

Toasty was the first to break the silence. "I have an idea," he said.

"That is quite unusual," boomed Indian Gook.

Toasty paid no attention to the rude interruption. "I got an idea that we could get in touch with Riley Goo."

"Riley who?" boomed the Gook.

"Not Riley Who," said Toasty. "It's Riley Goo."

"My, what a peculiar name," boomed the Gook. "Who, by the beard of the prophet is Riley Goo?"

"Riley Goo," answered Toasty, "is a professional man. He is the elevator starter at the Royal Crown Manor Imperial Palace Motel Hotel and part-time detective. I think we should hire him to find Doopey."

Upsty said, "At least we are getting on the right track, but Toasty, is this Riley Goo a good detective?"

"I have heard nothing but good concerning his tactics and there will be nothing lost in trying. We have to do something."

"Toasty is absolutely right," said Upsty. "Now how do we get in touch with Riley Goo?"

"Why not call him on the phone right now," said Toasty, "at the Royal Crown Manor Imperial Palace Motel Hotel?"

"Right, right you are," cried the impetuous Gook as he hurried over toward the phone.

Before he could make the call, however, Upsty stopped him. "It may not be a good idea to contact him on the phone," Upsty cautioned. "Suppose our wires are tapped. We wouldn't want to give our plans away to anyone who could be listening. I think it would be better if someone saw this Riley Goo in person. And why not you, Toasty? You know him."

"Without the impression of a doubt, you are right, Upsty. I know him and so does Doopey, which makes it even better."

So it was decided that Toasty would be the contact, and he hurried off on his very important mission. The last thing he heard was Indian Gook shouting about how much this detective was going to charge and Mary Jane screaming back about how could he think a thing like that at a time like this.

It was a sad little group that sat around the club room after Toasty left. They wondered where Doopey could be, and they wondered if this Riley Goo would be any help in locating him.

And then when the conversation was running out, the little girl spoke up. "I like your poemtree, Mr. Upsty," she said. "Could I see another of the poems?"

Before Upsty could answer, Glass was away like a shot and plucked one of the dangling pieces of paper from the poemtree. Glass read it to himself and then stopped and was taking it back to hang again on the poemtree when the little girl stopped him. She was excited and wondered why she couldn't see it. Glass did a lot of stammering, trying to explain about the time that Upsty fell in love with one of the people in the distant woods and that was when he wrote this poem.

"I don't think," said Glass, "that Upsty would want me to read it."

Upsty knew which poem he referred to and said, "Glass, that was long ago." He turned to the little girl. "I was very young then, and I had fallen madly in love. Things just didn't work out." If one looked close, it is possible that tears could be detected in Upsty's eyes.

"*Toujours gai*, Glass. Read the poem."

And Glass read:

We are two up in a cloud
Whisper, whisper, don't speak loud.
Gently, gently close the door
Tread the carpet, not the floor.
Whistle soft your mellow song
Stay awhile but not too long.
Keep the TV set down low
Ditto with the radio.
Please no coughing, do not sneeze
And no conversation please.
Oh, you're leaving spare the tears
Come again in twenty years
Then whisper, whisper, don't speak loud
We'll be two up in a cloud.

The little girl liked the poem, she thought, and Glass put it back on the poemtree. Then the members dispersed planning to come back the next day and discuss the missing Doopey and also the upcoming Happy Day party of the Jolly Club.

Riley Goo, a professional man, had once been a gas detective in Pennsylvania in a town called Wallopolitan. His job was to go around to buildings where there was chance that gas was leaking and then do something about it. One day, while he was making his rounds, there was an emergency call to go to a place in Shickshinny, which is across the Monongahela River from Wallopolitan, and certainly Riley Goo responded at once to the emergency. After rowing across the Monongahela River from Wallopolitan to Shickshinny, Riley Goo hastened to the place in question and entered speedily, forgetting in his concern the big cigar that he was smoking, and that was the reason for his early retirement.

Riley Goo was starting the elevators at the Royal Crown Imperial Palace Motel Hotel when he saw his friend Toasty approaching, and to Riley Goo it seemed that Toasty was quite distressed.

Toasty spoke first. "Riley Goo," he said, "this is an emergency."

Then he told Riley Goo of the disappearance of Doopey, and Riley Goo, the great detective, said, "My, my, my, my." And then he added, with a knowing look, "It's a kidnapping, that's what it is. You know what I mean? You know what I mean?"

"You're sure?" queried Toasty.

"Absogoshdarnlutely," answered the great detective. "But let us not tarry here, but let us go to the Jolly Club where we can talk to the members and tell them of our plans to recover the missing

Doopey. You know what I mean? You know what I mean?"

Toasty explained to Riley Goo that by this time all of the members would have left the clubhouse. So they departed, but not before making plans to meet the next day.

Second Quarter

Mary Jane was trying to walk over to see who was knocking at the secret door. Her legs acted as though they were made of rubber as she tried to duck around the others at this crazy party.

"Now who can this be?" she asked herself. "What kind of crazy character can this be?" Her rubbery legs finally got her to the door, and she opened it.

"Hello," said Mary Jane. "Come in and join the party."

"I will, I will, I will," cried the newcomer, who turned out to be Griddle Cake.

He came in and ran over to Sausage, and soon the two of them were dancing all around the floor. Mary Jane couldn't quite make out this party. It wasn't exactly as she had planned it, but she was having a good time watching all of these peculiar characters.

Fried Egg was singing a song, and Cup of Coffee was playing the piano. Bacon and Oatmeal were dancing, along with Sausage and Griddle Cake.

Cup of Coffee stopped playing the piano to make an announcement, but he couldn't make himself heard over the loud barking of the Hot

Dogs who were racing up and down and making a terrific noise. All the others had stopped dancing and singing and were waiting to hear the announcement that Cup of Coffee had to make. But it was impossible, just impossible, to be heard over the loud barking of the Hot Dogs.

It was at this point that Mary Jane woke up. "What a horrid dream," she said to herself, and then she laughed to think of a cup of coffee playing the piano and all of the other peculiar characters.

The barking that she heard in her dream continued, however, and she looked out of her window to see some real live dogs running and playing down the road. *There must be a dozen of them,* she thought and she recognized quite a few of them. There was Ben Gay and Mentholatum and Skippy and Alexander Patutnik. There were several dogs that Mary Jane did not recognize. But then she saw some of her real favorites. There was Sir Daffodil Magee, Winnie the Pooh, and last but not least along came Chang the Chinese dog. Now a funny thought came to Mary Jane. Could one of her favorites, Chang, be a Communist? But then she thought just because a dog is Chinese doesn't make him a Communist, and she dismissed the idea as being ridiculous.

Now whenever there was a big bunch of dogs, you could almost always depend that Indian Gook would be coming along and along he came.

Mary Jane yelled out the window to the giant Indian Gook that if he would wait a minute, she would join him and soon the two were skipping down the road on their way to the clubhouse, followed by a very noisy and curious-looking bunch of dogs.

The little girl once again was up bright and early on this beautiful summer morning, and once again she was on the porch playing with her dolls. She had no idea, of course, of the thrilling experience she was going to have before the day ended.

She looked occasionally across the street, past the old shanty, and into the field beyond it. Eventually she saw Mary Jane and Indian Gook coming along and following them, many, many dogs and, it seemed to her, of all sizes and varieties. The little girl hurried across the street and was about to enter the clubhouse when Toasty came along.

"Where did all the dogs come from, Toasty?" she asked.

"Followed the Gook, that's for sure," was the answer.

"But why do they follow Indian Gook?"

"Well, he's sort of their leader, I guess," said Toasty, laughing. "Yes, Princess, there's something about Indian Gook that attracts dogs. That's for sure." Toasty paused. "They follow him all around, everywhere."

"I think I like that funny-looking little black one best," said the Princess.

"And so did Doopey," said Toasty. "Do you want me to tell you about it?"

The Princess was sure she wanted to hear about it. She was excited to think that she and the missing Doopey liked the same dog.

"One day," Toasty said, "Doopey was going by the animal shelter and couldn't resist stopping in. Inside there was the dirtiest looking puppy that Doopey had ever seen. He felt sorry for the puppy and bought him and took him along with him."

"That was awfully nice of Mr. Doopey," said the Princess.

"Yes, it was, that's for sure," said Toasty.

There was a pause and then Toasty remembered, "When Upsty heard about what Doopey had done, he wrote a poem about the puppy, who they called Winnie the Pooh. It's somewhere on the poemtree and if I can find it, I will read it to you."

The Princess surely hoped that he could find the poem about Winnie the Pooh.

Now, Toasty and the Princess went into the clubhouse just as Mary Jane was calling the roll.

Of course Indian Gook tried to stop the little girl from attending the meeting and, of course, he was once again overruled and the little girl stayed. Mary Jane, as presiding officer, was very uppity at the meeting and after the roll call demanded to know what this Riley Goo was doing to find the missing Doopey. Also she would like to meet this Riley Goo.

"You'll meet him, that's for sure," said Toasty.

Mary Jane certainly hoped so, and then she thought that they had better start preparing for the Happy Day party, which was not far off.

"I think," said Mary Jane, "that Glass should do the shopping for the Happy Day goodies."

There was no opposition to her nomination, and so Glass was elected for the job.

"Could the Princess go with me?" asked Glass.

This question brought up arguments that probably never would have been settled, except that Upsty came up with the solution.

"Why not?" said Upsty. "Let the Princess go with him. As guardian. That way we would know that he would come back with the goodies." And they all laughed, for they all knew Glass's terrific appetite.

And so it was decided that the Princess would go with Glass on his shopping tour.

"Now," said Mary Jane, "that that is settled." She turned to Upsty. "How are you coming along with your song for the Jolly Club?"

Upsty explained that he hadn't had much time, what with all the excitement of the past few days. Doopey showed up missing and then the remarkable appearance of the little girl who they called Princess. Upsty promised he would have a song about the Jolly Club in time for the Happy Day party.

It was then that the members were startled by a knocking at the clubhouse door. And like the day before, confusion filled the clubhouse.

Toasty suddenly remembered that the great detective, Riley Goo, was to make an appearance at the clubhouse, and so he went over and opened the door. Sure enough, there he was in person, Riley Goo.

The members ooh'd and aah'd to think that they had such a famous person among them. And the great detective entered bowing to all of the members and after each introduction, he stated that it was his pleasure, "To be sure, you know what I mean."

Then Toasty asked the detective if he had anything to report about the missing Doopey.

"I do, indeed I do," said Riley Goo. And then a strange scared look came on his face, as though a hundred lions were about to devour him. Riley Goo's voice rose and fell like one syllable would be away up on the roof and the next one would be away down in the basement. With the terrorized look on his face and the rising and falling of his voice, poor Upsty had a hard time to keep from laughing when the detective said, "The operation is a lot bigger than we first suspected." But, of course, Upsty didn't laugh because of the seriousness of the situation.

Poor Mary Jane was horror-struck as though she, too, had seen the hundred lions. "Mr. Goo," she sobbed, "are you going to get our poor Doopey back?"

"Of course I will, of course I will." Riley Goo tried to cry out loudly, but only every other syllable made it. He looked at Mary Jane as if to say, how could you ever doubt that I would succeed.

Then Riley Goo remembered he had to make a phone call in connection with the mystery and without asking permission dashed across the room and used the club's phone. All of the members were trying to hear what the detective was saying, but they heard only a few words, and the ones they did, like mizzenmast and batten the hatches, didn't make much sense to them. And right before he hung up, they heard him say, "Anchors aweigh, you know what I mean."

And then Riley Goo left, but not before attempting to cry out, "A new development has developed. You know what I mean."

After his departure there was much babbling among the members. Upsty said he wasn't much impressed with Riley Goo and the others, hearing that, became even more depressed and wondered if they would ever see poor Doopey again. They were indeed a sad looking bunch.

And then Toasty looked over and happened to see the little girl, who, like the others, was finding it hard to hold back the tears. Toasty remembered the poem that Upsty had written about one of the dogs that constantly trailed Indian Gook, and he had promised the Princess that he would try to find it on the poemtree. After searching for a few minutes he finally found it and took it over and read it to the Princess.

The Story of My Life
(or it shouldn't happen to a dog)

Very many years ago when I was just a pup
I lived in such a mangy place that I could just
    throw up
At any little mention of that dank and dirty cell
And of the caged-up prisoners whining in their hell.
A man looked through the bars one day and said, I
    guess she'll do,
And paid three bucks and took me home and
    named me Win the Pooh.
Then started education of the kind you will agree
Was really not essential for a dog as smart as me.
"Sleep here, sleep there, do this, do that,
Go in, stay out, don't chase the pussy cat."
I tried to live, I really did by all their foolish rules
How was a dog to understand that they were ruling
    fools?
But gradually I understood they tried their stupid
    best
To make of me a family pet and not a doggone pest.
And gradually I undertook, although it was quite
    rude
To try a little trick or two like stealing of their food.
But that was many years ago when I was but a pup
And reason can develop when a dog is growing up.
I learned the stupid things they did, they did them
    just for me
For they considered Win The Pooh one of the family.

The Princess felt bad about the way they had the puppy caged up in that awful place, but she was happy that Doopey had seen him and made it possible that the puppy would be free.

"I think I like Upsty's poem," she said.

"Well, unregardless of whether you did or not, back it goes up on the poemtree," and Toasty skipped across the room and hung up Upsty's poem.

Glass went over to the Princess at this time and thought that they should get ready for their shopping expedition, and the little girl agreed. And soon the two of them were hurrying down the street to the market place.

Intermission

The members of the Jolly Club often reminisced about one particular birthday that Upsty celebrated. As was the custom among the members, Upsty gave a gift to each of the other members.

Doopey made his formal acknowledgment of thanks for the gift he had received and was surprised a few days later to receive the following from Upsty:

> I was very pleased you wrote,
> Thank you for your thank-you note.

Doopey immediately sat down and penned the following:

> Thank you for the card you wrote
> To thank me for my thank-you note.

Now it was Upsty's turn, and he pondered and finally wrote:

> You'll never know how much it meant
> To get the lovely note you sent
> That thanked me for the card I wrote

To thank you for your thank you note.

That will end that, thought Upsty, but he underestimated Doopey, and a few days later he received these lines:

I never thought I'd ever get
A note as nice as yours and yet
It gives me every kind of chance
To offer you my utmost thanks—
So thank you kindly for the note
That thanked me for the card I wrote
To thank you for the thanks you wrote
To thank me for my thank you note.

After that, Upsty gave up.

Second Half

The little girl was laughing like perhaps she had never laughed before in her whole five years. And at the same time, the little girl was almost in tears. She was laughing because as Glass was buying all of the goodies for the Happy Day party, he sampled everything he bought. The little girl looked at his tummy and wondered why it wasn't bigger than it was.

The little girl was near tears too because her arms were weary from carrying all of the packages that Glass bought. Everything he purchased he handed to the little girl, and she was almost lost in a sea of packages.

Sampling all of the goodies was not enough for Glass. He took the Princess into a restaurant and treated her to a dish of spaghetti. The little girl could not finish her meal, but she looked on in amazement as Glass ate three large helpings.

With all of the goodie-sampling and the three large orders of spaghetti, poor Glass was in an awful way. He just couldn't navigate the way he wanted to. His tummy was double its usual size as he got up and left the table. At this point, he bumped into a tall lean object and when seeing this object swaying, he quickly grabbed it at about the middle to try to steady it. Glass suddenly had a funny feeling, and he looked up to see a tall thin stranger looking down at him in amazement, for Glass was holding the stranger by the hips, steadying him so that he would not fall down.

Now the little girl laughed, and laughed, and laughed, for she had never seen anything so funny in her whole life Glass holding this tall thin man by the hips to keep him from falling down. And when the little girl thought that there was no more laugh left in her, Glass looked up and saw the stranger and realized what he was doing he was panic stricken.

"Pardon me," he cried out. "I thought you were a hat rack." The stranger stared at Glass in disbelief and Glass, unable to gain his composure, ran streaking from the restaurant. The little girl tried to keep up with him, but it was difficult, for she was laughing so hard there were tears in her eyes.

All of the members except Doopey, of course, were at the clubhouse when Glass and the Princess returned with all of their packages.

Upsty had just announced that he had finished the Jolly Club song, and some of the members were "practizing" it, but they stopped when Glass and the Princess came in and they put up the newly purchased decorations for the Happy Day party.

Now all of them, including the Princess, joined in singing the new Jolly Club song.

Upsty was real proud of the song that he had composed and the words were his all right, but the music had a sort of familiar ring, as though Upsty had been listening to a lot of Gilbert and Sullivan lately.

THE JOLLY CLUB SONG

We are the members of the Jolly Club
The jolly jolly members of the Jolly Club
We sing a lot—we dance a lot
And whether the weather is cold or hot
We have fun and we cannot
Worry 'bout the money that we ain't got.
We are the members of the Jolly Club
The jolly jolly members of the Jolly Club
We are friends through thick and thin
When things look dark we wear a grin
And fight our battles until we win.
And we ain't afeared of nothin' of course but sin.

Oh, we are the members of the Jolly Club
The jolly jolly members of the Jolly Club
On HAPPY DAY we have a ball
It's all for one and one for all
Yes, all for one and one for all
Through the summer and the winter and spring
and fall.

And after a little while of singing, the Princess, after the biggest day of her life, begged off and decided that she had better be going home. And as she left she waved to her friends who thanked her profusely for helping Glass do all the shopping.

The members kept harmonizing their new song until they were interrupted by the ringing of the phone. Upsty went over to answer it while the other members waited in hushed silence.

"Hello," said Upsty. "Who is calling?"

"This," was the reply in a strange rising and falling voice, "is the great detective, Riley Goo."

"Yes, yes?" asked Upsty. "Is there anything new?"

"I have," announced the great detective and there was a long pause, "I have found the missing Doopey."

When Upsty hung up the phone and told of his conversation with Riley Goo, of course there was much joyous exclaiming in the clubhouse. It was a wonder that the roof, as bad as it was, didn't fly off with all of the howling and screaming.

After the hubbubing had mostly subsided, Upsty was able to tell his friends the rest of his talk with Riley Goo. "The great detective, who has found our Doopey, wants us to meet him here very early tomorrow morning, and then he will direct us to where our missing friend is."

Then the meeting ended and the members left, knowing that it would be hard for them to wait until the next morning.

Some days are made for staying in the house, and some are made for going out in the fresh air.

Some days are made for exploring the forests with their brooks and streams and giant trees. This was the kind of day it was when the members met early in the morning to go to find their friend Doopey.

Riley Goo was quite impatient. He had arrived much earlier than the others and was anxious to get started, for he explained they had a long walk ahead of them.

"I think," spoke out Riley Goo, "that we should go in two separate parties. You know what I mean."

They looked at him as though they didn't know what he meant, and he explained.

"I'm pretty certain I know where Doopey is," he said, "but there is always the question of gaining his release."

"His release?" questioned Upsty. "Do you mean he is being held for ransom?"

"Well, let us put it this way," answered the detective. "A ransom may be demanded. You know what I mean."

"But, but," cried out Mary Jane, "what would we use for ransom? Oh, oh, this is awful."

And now Mary Jane's friends joined her lamenting.

But Riley Goo shushed them up. "You didn't let me finish," he said. "I think that we can get him back without paying any ransom, but we must be very cautious. They are a dangerous gang." Riley Goo paused to catch his breath. "I think the safest way for us to travel is in two separate parties.

Upsty, divide the members into two groups. One group should follow me down the low road, and the other group should follow you up the high road. You know what I mean. Some up the high road and some down the low road. You know what I mean."

And Riley Goo, for some reason known only to himself, laughed out and that was a funny sound, for none of the members had ever heard Riley Goo laugh before. It was more like a frantic sort of giggle than a laugh, and it made the members shudder a little bit.

And eventually they set out on their quest. Upsty and Glass and Mary Jane went up the high road when they got into the forest. Toasty and Indian Gook followed the great detective down the low road.

Some distance away—it would probably take at least two hours—the two roads met and it was there, Riley Goo explained, where they would find the missing Doopey.

This was a new part of the dense woods for the members of the club. They had almost always gone in the opposite direction.

Halfway along the high road, Mary Jane complained that her feet hurt. Glass, too, had a very hard time keeping up with Upsty, probably because of all that spaghetti the day before among other things.

The other group, led by Riley Goo, had little trouble on the low road. In fact they arrived where the two roads met about half an hour before the other group.

And while waiting Riley Goo cautioned them to be quiet.

"We must not under any circumstance," said the detective, "louse up the soup. You know what I mean." They didn't exactly know what he meant, but they kept quiet until finally they were joined by the others.

Now Riley Goo took command.

"Follow me, follow me," he cried out, the syllables rising and falling, and he dashed out like it was the Charge of the Light Brigade.

About half an hour passed, and the group came upon a wide open area. Riley Goo announced that this was the place. Here they would find Doopey.

But there was no Doopey to be seen anywhere, and Riley Goo said, "We have waited long enough. Now we strike. You know what I mean." And then, "Follow me."

They all followed the great detective, and they went through many roads and lanes, but there was still no Doopey. And then the great detective made the statement that astonished them all. And scared them too. In a voice even more shaky even than usual, he started to cry, "I think we're lost. I think we're lost. You know what I mean."

Mary Jane was exhausted. She started to cry. "I'm exhausted," she wailed out, "I'm exhausted."

The others tried to soothe her. Indian Gook said, “Mary Jane, don’t cry. Remember we will all die of starvation together.” That was just what Mary Jane didn’t need, and the tears flowed faster.

Upsty could stand no more of this. He tried to calm his friends and said, “We should all hang together or else we surely will all hang separately.” A guilty feeling flashed through Upsty’s mind. He was sure he hadn’t made up that “hang together” thing. He had read it somewhere or else someone had said it to him.

Another hour passed and Riley Goo and the others were visibly upset. Mary Jane, of course, was still crying, and the others it seemed were trying to catch up to her. There just didn’t seem to be any possible way out of this dense forest.

Sometimes when the sky is darkest and there is no sign of blue visible anywhere, if you have faith, something good will surely happen. And the club members didn’t give up, and they remembered the line in the new Jolly Song, “When things look dark, we wear a grin,” and they sang as loud as they possibly could.

And they weren’t disappointed, for suddenly as they were singing, they heard a voice that seemed to come from far above in the sky.

“Follow me, follow me. I will see that you get free,” came the voice from high above.

It was getting quite dusk now, and the club members were glad to follow anyone who could get them out of this horrible jungle. And so they

followed this stranger who had slid down a giant tree and promised that he would free them.

Riley Goo followed closely behind the newcomer, and the members of the club were behind him, having a very difficult time in the dense woods, for it was getting darker by the minute. After what seemed like a dozen hours, but of course was not that long, of plodding through many, many roads and lanes and over streams and brooks, they eventually came upon the field they knew so well. And there, in the not too-far-distance, they could see in the darkness the outline of the clubhouse, a very beautiful sight indeed.

They were all exhausted when they went inside and as though they had been practicing it, they all practically collapsed on the floor at the same time, forgetting in their overtired condition the stranger who had rescued them.

Toasty was the first one of the weary group who came back out of the land of dreams and at first started to look around not too sure where he was. Then he saw the overstuffed chair behind the poemtree and the little fellow sitting in it. Then Toasty rubbed his eyes in disbelief. It wasn't Upsty as usual sitting in the chair. No, indeed, it was not Upsty but their rescuer.

And, of course, dear readers, you have all guessed that this rescuer was the beloved, long-missing Doopey.

"Doopey, Doopey," cried out Toasty, so loud that the other members woke up and got to their feet so fast that you would think the clubhouse had suddenly been hit by a bomb. When the members got all of the sleep out of their eyes and saw Doopey, delirium took over. There certainly had never been a scene before in the clubhouse like the one that was exploding now.

Doopey was hugged and kissed, and the members were screaming as they tried to get near him. They laughed and cried at the same time, and when Doopey was able to free himself of them, he led the group in singing the new Jolly Club song.

And after much singing, Indian Gook bellowed out, "We went to rescue you, but it wound up by you rescuing us." They all laughed at this, and then there was another round of hugging Doopey and singing.

When all played out, they left the clubhouse and went their separate ways, promising to meet the following day for the great celebration of Happy Day and also Doopey's safe return.

That night, the little girl who lived in the white house had a very peculiar dream. She dreamt they had found Doopey sitting high up on top of the poemtree.

The following day was as beautiful as the one preceding it. All of the members were at the clubhouse, and they were dressed in their gayest colors, for today was Happy Day and they were having their big party.

The little girl who lived across the street in the white house came in. She met Doopey, and that was the biggest day she ever had, even bigger than when she went shopping with Glass.

And what a time they all had. There was every kind of food imaginable, and there was dancing and there was singing, and the song that they sang most was Upsty's new Jolly Club song.

Then at one point, when a little silence broke in, Upsty said he wanted to ask Doopey a question.

"Doopey," he asked, "how just how in the world did you do it?"

"Well," said Doopey, "it happened like this." All of the members circled around to hear Doopey's story.

"You remember, Upsty, long, long ago out in the deep woods, I was left all alone. There was no one to look after me. I was no more than three years old."

"I remember," said Upsty, "how well I remember, and one day I came along and found you, and after that I was sorta like your big brother. But, what has that got to do with the great practical joke you played on us?"

"Well, it was like this," said Doopey, "you remember, of course, the old house in the deep woods that for generations belonged to my ancestors." Upsty nodded and Doopey continued. "I often went there, but not in the past few years.

Then, one day a couple of months ago, I was near the old place and thought that I would go over and I did. There were hundreds of old books that my forefathers had brought over from the old country. I used to go over there and read them a lot, but I hadn't for years. On this occasion I picked up one that I had never read before."

Doopey paused for refreshments, and Upsty said he couldn't quite figure out what Doopey was getting at.

Then Doopey continued. "I was looking through the yellowed pages of this old book and came upon this poem:

> Shawn O'Shaughnessy, misguided Leprechaun
> Dreamed that the forest he loved so had up and gone,
> Dreamed that the green grass he once loved to play upon
> Had vanished and so had the misguided Leprechaun.

"When I read that," continued Doopey, "I got my idea for the practical joke. I would disappear and I had it figured out just what would happen. First, there would be a lot of hysterical moments at the clubhouse, and then there would be meetings to determine a course of action to pursue to find the missing Doopey. Some sort of mysterious phone call to the clubhouse would make you all realize how serious the situation was and that you should engage a detective."

"Right you are, Doopey," Upsty interrupted, "and we did just that. We hired Riley Goo."

"Yes," said Doopey with an impish grin, "but I got in touch with Riley Goo first. You see, that was part of the plan. I knew that when you thought of hiring a detective, Toasty would think of his friend, Riley Goo."

Upsty laughed. "And it all worked out the way you planned it, Doopey. It has to be one of the greatest hoaxes ever perpetrated. But you had us worried a lot, Doopey."

"I know, I know," said Doopey, "I didn't like that part of it. But I just couldn't resist the temptation. And now if you will forgive me, we will continue with the great Happy Day party."

And they all did, with more eating and singing and dancing, and it seemed to the Princess that the party would never end. She hoped that it wouldn't.

But it did, of course, "unregardless" of the wishes of the Princess.

Overtime

He was little with long, sandy hair. He was almost lost in a large, overstuffed chair, hiding behind a tall, artificial tree. The tree had raggedy pieces of paper dangling from its make-believe branches.

He was sound asleep and snoring happily away. There was a pencil in his right hand and a tablet in his lap. He was away off in the Land of Nod, but his right hand holding the pencil was busily writing away on the tablet. He finally woke up and his misty eyes saw the tablet. He read the poem he had just written.

Nothing quite so aggravating
As this Miss who keeps me waiting,
And then, when finally she meets me
Seldom lingers once she greets me.

No wonder often in confusion
I think her a sweet illusion.
Could it be that fancy's playing
Tricks that cause a mental straying?

Then I see those blue eyes flirtin'
She is real I know for certain.
And I touch the gold hair streaming
Surely then I am not dreaming.

Ho, she comes now, swishes walking
And she'll lisp a little talking.
Exquisitely her charms so sweetly
Fit into my arms and neatly.

But whoops she's gone now, begs my pardon
Skips away to kindergarten.

After the little sandy-haired man finished reading his new poem, he surmised that a certain five-year-old girl had stopped in to see him on her way to school. Then he took his new creation over to hang it on the poemtree. But then he paused, scratched his head, and then signed his name to the poem. He took it across the street and put it in the mailbox of the white house. Then the little man went back to the shanty, removed all of the dangling pieces of paper from the poemtree, and stuffed them in his pockets. A few minutes later, he was away over the field and into the dense forest.

That afternoon the man in the white house across from the old shanty was startled when taking the mail from the mailbox to find a poem that was signed by one of his daughter's make-believe friends. His daughter had told him of her strange playmates, and he had laughed, of course, but now he read the poem and he wondered, and wondered, and wondered.

A few days later, some workmen came and tore down the old shack. But as the little girl was growing up, for years she could still see it there. In her imagination she could still see her friends coming across the field to the clubhouse.